MacGregor, Carol Lynn

Shoshoni pony

Shoshoni Pony

SHOSHONI PONY

by

Carol Lynn MacGregor, PhD

with illustrations by

Dick Lee

CAXTON PRESS

Library of Congress Cataloging-in-Publication Data

MacGregor, Carol Lynn, 1942-
  Shoshoni pony : first horse in the Northwest / by Carol Lynn MacGregor ; with illustrations by Dick Lee.
    p. cm.
  Summary: An overview of how horses came to be used by various peoples in the American West, particularly the Shoshoni Indians, discussing the difference that horses made in their lives.
  ISBN 0-87004-431-1 (alk. paper)
  1. Shoshoni Indians—Juvenile literature. 2. Horses—Northwest, Pacific—History—Juvenile literature.   [1. Shoshoni Indians. 2. Indians of North America—West (U.S.) 3. Horses.]   I. Lee, Dick, 1929-   , ill. II. Title.
E99.S4M3 2003
978.004'9745—dc21

2002011093

Lithographed and bound for
Caxton Press
Caldwell, Idaho
168880

Printed in China

The prehistoric horses found in fossils along the Snake River were extinct when people came to live in the land that is now the northwestern United States. For thousands of years while American Indians lived on this land, there were no horses.

The Northern Shoshoni and many other tribes used dogs to move their camps. They moved from place to place to find food. The people carried things on their backs, and their dogs sometimes pulled travois. Packs were placed on poles that allowed the dogs to pull larger burdens than they could carry on their backs. These native peoples of the deserts, hills, and valleys of the Northwest could not transport many goods with them. They could not move very quickly on foot.

Before they got horses, Shoshoni people had to hunt and gather food on foot. They devised many tools to help them obtain food. For instance, they made snares to trap rabbits and squirrels in the desert. Along the rivers, they fished with spears and with hooks they dangled from poles with reed line. They dried their fish to save and use when food became scarce. They gathered berries in the summer. The berries were used to flavor food, eat raw, or dry to eat later. Another great food source were the tiny but nutritious pine nuts that they gathered in the early autumn.

The Shoshoni knew how to follow the signs of the seasons to find food. It took a lot of time and effort just to move camp to find enough food for the people to eat.

They knew how to hide from their enemies although sometimes they were ambushed by surprise. They knew how to gather and hunt food on foot. Their lives were not easy, but they survived this way for thousands of years in an area where it often was very hot in the summer and very cold in the winter.

Far to the South at Santa Fe, which is now in New Mexico, lived Spaniards and other American Indians. Some of the native people were "sedentary." They stayed in one place and lived in towns made of adobe mud. Others were "nomadic" and roved about, changing their camps with the seasons like the Shoshoni.

The Pueblo Indians, who lived in the adobe villages were able to practice religions with complex rituals in underground kivas and make beautiful pottery because they lived in one place. In 1598, Spaniards moved into the area on the Rio Grande River to a place now near Santa Fe, New Mexico. The Spaniards lived near one of the Indian towns.

The Spaniards brought men, women, children, horses, pigs, cows and other animals from Europe that were not familiar to Indians of America. The Spaniards forced Pueblo tribes to work for them and learn their religion for about eighty years. During this time, many Indians learned how to ride the Spanish horses, descendants of horses called "the Arab Barbs" from North Africa. Besides the Pueblo Indians who worked for the Spaniards on horses, the Navajo and the Apache Indians sometimes captured the Spaniards' horses and learned how to ride them.

Many of the Pueblos were not happy working for the Spaniards. In 1680, Pueblo people from different towns joined together and fought the Spaniards. They drove them out of Santa Fe, south to El Paso, now in Texas.

In 1680 when the Spaniards fled south, they left many of their horses. The Comanches, Navajos and Apaches captured some of the Spanish horses from the Pueblos. Some of these tribes already had small numbers of horses they had captured or traded earlier. But when the Pueblo Revolt happened, large numbers of horses became available to the tribes of the Southwest. The Pueblo Revolt changed horse ownership in a dramatic way. Many more Indians could now have a lot more horses. They began to trade these horses to other tribes. Tribes traded the horses from the New Mexican area to the north and to the east.

The Comanche tribe and the Shoshoni tribe were the same people and could understand each other's language. The Comanches took horses northward and traded them with the Shoshoni. By 1700, Northern Shoshoni Indians had horses they got from the Comanches. The Shoshonis became the first people in the Northwest to have horses. They soon learned how to handle the horses, how to ride them, train them and use them to improve their lives. The Shoshoni became good trainers and riders of horses.

Using horses, the Shoshoni people could ride far to hunt buffalo. They rode their horses very fast next to the buffalo and shot them with arrows. Then they used their horses to carry the heavy buffalo back to camp.

All parts of the buffalo were very useful to the tribe, including the meat, the bones, horns, skin, organs, and even the hooves. They ate the meat, boiled the bones for broth, made containers from the bladders, and fashioned decorations, tools, and bells from the horns and hooves. From the skin, they made clothing, rawhide ropes to handle their horses, and larger tipis that horses could carry when the tribe moved from place to place.

Being the first tribe in the Northwest to have horses helped the Shoshoni people. They could move their camps much easier than when they had to travel on foot. They could carry many possessions in larger loads on their horses. They could move faster to hunt buffalo, to move camp, and to scout for danger.

With horses, they could better escape from their enemies. Having horses gave the Shoshoni more power with other tribes. They could trade for other items that they needed.

In 1805 white men first visited the Northern Shoshoni people in Idaho. They came to find out what the land looked like between the Missouri River and the Pacific Ocean. Meriwether Lewis and William Clark led this first group of explorers.

When they led their exploration party to Idaho, Lewis and Clark brought an American Indian girl, Sacagawea, and her baby with them. She was a Northern Shoshoni and the only female on the trip. Her husband was a French trader whom Lewis and Clark met at Fort Mandan in present-day North Dakota. Sacagawea came home to her people in the mountains where the land is now called eastern Idaho. Her brother, Cameahwait, was the chief of the Lemhi band of Shoshoni.

Lewis and Clark and their men saw Cameahwait's tribe had many fine horses. They wrote that the Shoshoni horses were as fine as those in Virginia where they came from. They noted that the Shoshoni people rode excellently through very rough country.

Lewis and Clark's exploration party needed horses to cross the mountains before winter. They needed to talk to the chief to trade for horses. Sacagawea helped to translate language between her brother, the chief, and Lewis so that they could buy horses from her tribe. There were five people in the translation chain. Lewis spoke English to a man named Labiche, who spoke French to Charbonneau. Charbonneau spoke Hidatsa Indian language to Sacagawea, who spoke Shoshoni to her brother.

The Lewis and Clark Expedition had to obtain horses in order to cross the snowy Bitterroot Mountains to reach the Pacific Ocean before winter. The Shoshoni traded many horses for items that the Americans had that were new to them. They also furnished Lewis and Clark with a guide named Tobe who would show them the way across the mountains.

Several of the men on the Lewis and Clark expedition wrote journals, so that we can read today about the horses that the Shoshoni in Idaho had 200 years ago. The explorers traded guns, jackets, buttons, needles, blankets, mirrors, cooking utensils and other items to get the horses they needed. The journalists wrote that the Shoshoni people had many fine horses. They wrote that Shoshonis were very good horseback riders.

Having horses greatly changed the lives of the Northern Shoshoni people. It changed the way that they moved their camps, hunted, prepared their clothing and their tipis. It changed warfare and made it easier for them to trade with other tribes. Many other tribes in the Northwest got horses from the Shoshoni, including the Blackfeet, Nez Perce, Cayuse, Spokan, and Bannock.

Horses became the source of their wealth, security, and well being. Horses really changed the lives of the people. Shoshoni were the first people in the Northwest to have the horse.

Glossary

American Indians — people native to the Americas.

Cameahwait — chief of the Lemhi Shoshoni and relative, probably brother, to Sacagawea.

Camps — temporary places where natives lived.

Comanches — nomadic tribe of south central plains; Spanish name for southern Shoshoni people.

Exploration party— a group that goes to explore new land.

Lewis and Clark — leaders of an exploration party between 1804 and 1806 to the West.

Navajos — a tribe of American Indians who live in the Southwest.

Possessions — things that people own.

Pueblo Indians — several tribal groups that lived in little towns of adobe houses when the Spaniards arrived to the Southwest. They practiced the same customs and live in present-day New Mexico and Arizona.

Sacagawea — a Lemhi Shoshoni girl who was captured by Hidatsa Indians and taken to the Hidatsa village in North Dakota where the exploration party of Lewis and Clark met her the winter of 1804-05. She accompanied her husband, Charbonneau, with their baby Jean Baptiste to the Pacific Ocean with Lewis and Clark and their men.

Snares — traps that caught small animals.

Spaniards — people who came from Spain.

Tipis — portable homes in which American Indians lived made of brush or skins.

Translate — change one language into another.

Information for this book has been obtained from extensive research, including the following:

Alden R. Carter, *The Shoshoni*, New York: Franklin Watts, 1989.

Elwyn Hartley Edwards, ed., *Enclyclopedia of the Horse*, London: Octopus Books Ltd., 1977.

Dennis B. Fradin, *The Shoshoni*, Chicago: Children's Press, 1988.

Francis D. Haines, "The Northward Spread of Horses Among the Plains Indians," *American Anthropologist* 40:3 (July-September 1938).

Carol Lynn MacGregor, *The Journals of Patrick Gass of the Lewis and Clark Expedition*. Missoula, Montana: Mountain Press, 1997.

Gary E. Moulton, *The Journals of the Lewis and Clark Expedition*. Vol. 1-10. Lincoln: University of Nebraska Press. 1986-1998.

James Ronda, *Lewis and Clark Among the Indians*. Lincoln: University of Nebraska Press, 1984.

Deward E. Walker, Jr., *Indians of Idaho*. Moscow, Idaho: University of Idaho Press, 1978.

Wyman D. Walker, *The Wild Horse of the West*, Caldwell, Idaho: Caxton Printers, Ltd., 1945.

Don Worcester, *The Spanish Mustang*, El Paso, Texas: Texas Western Press, 1986.